Secrets of Music

A collection of articles

UDC 141.339=111=03.161.1
BBC 87.7+86.4
M 59

M 59 Mickushina, T.N.
Secrets of Music: A collection of articles
Comp. by: T. N. Mickushina, E. Y. Ilyina. -
Black/white ill.-(Series "Spiritual & Moral Culture")
2017. – 90 pages.

Our whole life is permeated with sounds, with music. The quality of music is a very important factor on which the further course of evolution directly depends.

What is the quality of the music that constantly accompanies our lives: in stores, in cafes, from televisions and radios? Music can heal or it can literally destroy.

This collection of articles reveals secrets of music. Having knowledge of the effects of music on us and on our environment, we can consciously apply this knowledge and drastically change our lives!

ISBN-10: 1973908840
ISBN-13: 978-1973908845

Contents

Preface 5

Music forever 9

Everything that exists is music 16

Sound, rhythm, music and their
influence on humans 25

Rock music destroys everything 38

Music is a weapon! 43

About music therapy 59

Quotations about Music from
the books "Words of Wisdom"................................. 75

Preface

"In the beginning was the Word…" that is how the Gospel of John begins.

Many philosophical systems state that Creation started with a vibration, with a sound.

Our entire life is permeated with sounds. Even the whole visible world, everything that surrounds us, is condensed sound or music.

The modern science of Synergetics asserts that it is the slight, subtle impacts that have the greatest influence on the world. Music is an example of such impacts. In this regard let us recall the words of the great Lao Tzu: the softest things in the world overcome the hardest things in the world.

The quality of music is a very important factor, which, without exaggeration, affects the further course of evolution of humanity.

Our world is dual, and every manifestation in it has two sides: good and evil, love and hate, white and black.

Music can also be of various types. It can heal, and it can also literally destroy.

The ancients possessed knowledge of how music affects the consciousness of man and society. The secret knowledge was kept by the priests in the temples. Only some of the secrets of music were passed down to us.

Thus, the ancient Greek philosopher Plato wrote: "Musical education is a more effective means than any other because rhythm and harmony find their way into the depth of the soul...the introduction of new kinds of music should be avoided — it endangers the entire country because a change in the musical style is always accompanied by the influence on the most important political areas."

Pythagoras believed music to be irreplaceable for the health of the soul, morality, and the flourishing of culture. Aristotle affirmed: "Music has power to form character; by music a man becomes accustomed to feeling the right emotions".

Outstanding English pianist and composer of the 20th century Cyril Scott claimed that it was music that created cultural epochs (not vice versa) and that every kind of music had a significant influence on the history, morality, and culture of mankind.

We can trace how the rhythm of music was changing and becoming more and more rapid in the 20th century; along with this, the rhythm of our lives was also changing. Nowadays it is often compared to a rat race. With the appearance of new-fangled styles of music, the worldview of society was also changing:

the overall level of culture decreased and moral guidelines changed.

Today music has become an integral part of our lives: It flows continuously from televisions and radios; it accompanies us when we do our shopping; and it can be heard in every restaurant, café, and club. But what is the quality of this music that enthralls space? How does it affect our health and condition? Does it inspire creativity, beauty, and divine refinement or does it take us under its control, brainwash us, and force us to make the wrong decisions?

Our collection of articles[1] reveals secrets of music. Having knowledge about the impact of music on us and on the world around us, we can consciously apply this knowledge and change our lives drastically!

The compilers of the digest.

---

[1] The articles in this collection are given in abridged form.

Music forever

Music is always present in our lives; it sounds within us. It has been established that an individual frequency is inherent in every person, coinciding with the frequency of one of the seven notes. Melodies, causing the listener to experience positive emotions, increase the activity of the cerebral cortex, improve the metabolism, and stimulate breathing and blood circulation. Music affects a person regardless of his consciousness.

It is known that the power of Orpheus' art conquered not only people but also gods and even nature. On one of the peaks of the Rhodope Mountains, Orpheus built a sacred temple, Odeon, the remains of which were found in the middle of the 20th century in the territory of modern Bulgaria, near the town of Plovdiv. In this temple Orpheus cured all incoming patients by using music and singing. Similarly, when the famous Italian singer Farinelli was invited to see the Spanish king Philip in 1730, after listening to Farinelli's singing, the king miraculously got rid of the chronic diseases and depression tormenting him.

American scientists at the Jet Propulsion laboratory in Pasadena discovered the phenomenon of "sound emission." Directing powerful ultrasounds into a glass jar with water, they saw how tiny bubbles were formed, emitting bluish light. This phenomenon proves the reality of the physical effects of sound on matter, not only audible but also those that are inaudible to the human ear.

Music can be picked up not only by the ear but it can also penetrate directly into the body in the form of sound waves. The vibrational nature of sound and music creates a language that our body and mind understand. In this case the word "language" means not the words but information. In this context the word "information" comes from the Latin "informare," which means "form." In other words, music is a process of changing acoustic forms. If we could see the forms created by music, we would see structures like the mountains, valleys, trees, micro-organisms, and galaxies. The study of the forms created by music is called Cymatics. Scientists have already collected numerous photos of Cymatic drawings, which appear when sound vibrations are transmitted through a metal plate with various resonating objects, such as metal shavings or sand. These studies have shown that music creates a certain kind of language. The order of the information (notes) in music is just as important as the order of the information (words) in speech. This identification of music as a language opens science to new possibilities of understanding the influence of music on the brain.

Any sound vibration consists of waveforms — the higher the frequency, the higher the pitch. The normal frequency range for a human ear is from 20 to 20 thousand Hz. Some people can hear sounds above 20 thousand Hz, but very few people can hear below 20 Hz. Using different frequencies, we can cause certain parts of the body to resonate, activating various processes.

Music — its rhythm, timbre and tone — can significantly affect the brain. A fast tempo causes increased circulation of blood and other bodily fluids, changes the heart rate, and increases emotional activity. A slow tempo has the opposite effect.

There was also a connection established between the frequency of sound waves and the success of training. Dr. Lozanov from Bulgaria was able to achieve an acceleration of the learning process in the course of his experiments by utilizing music with a tempo of 60 beats per minute (i.e., baroque music). Later, Dr. Lozanov's method became well-known in America as a method of accelerated learning. Dr. Sue Chapman studied the effect of music on premature babies. One group of infants was played Brahms' "Lullaby" six times a day, while the other group did not listen to any music. Newborns who listened to Brahms gained weight faster, suffered from fewer complications, and were discharged from the hospital on average one week earlier than "non-musical" babies.

The intensity or power of sound, undoubtedly, has a profound effect on the body, especially on the nervous system. Each of us has had the opportunity to observe this phenomenon more than once in our lives. The intensity of sound for normal perception is in the range of approximately 50 to 90 decibels. Some rock music, for example, can reach up to 115 decibels, while the pain threshold is in the range of 125 decibels. Moreover, the same sound can sound differently depending on the timbre. That is, the waveform can be different even when the frequency is the same; it is this difference that can influence us. Dr. Ohno of the Beckman Research Institute in Duarte, California, managed to pick up a musical note from each of the amino acids that make up the DNA code. He recorded the music "played" by the DNA helix of various living creatures. It turned out that these were not isolated sounds but real melodies. In one of his experiments, Dr. Ohno recorded the melody of a certain type of cancer cells. It was strikingly similar to the "Funeral March" by Chopin.

Positive emotional experiences, when someone is listening to the sounds of pleasant music, tone the central nervous system and enhance the attention. A skillfully chosen melody can reduce fatigue and improve health. At the same time, additional nerve cells get involved in neural activity and share the load with other units already running in the system. Recent studies have also shown that under the influence of classical music, significant changes take place in the blood, decreasing the number of hormones that cause overstrain of the nervous system. Simultaneously, an increase occurs in the concentration of one of the components in the blood which is the most important element of the immune system in protecting the body against viruses.

Renowned researcher Dr. Campbell strongly recommends for those who experience stress overload at work to listen to classical music daily for 15 minutes.

These are but a few examples of the beneficial effects of music. According to Chinese physicians of the hospital in Tianjin, music helps patients to overcome fear of going on the operating table during simple surgical procedures. Initially music was played during surgeries to relieve the stress on surgeons. They noticed that it helped patients to calm down and become distracted from the unpleasant procedure. Now, any patient can order the music of his choice before surgery.

However, music not only heals, it can also destroy. We should not blame music for this, but ourselves. Nowadays even the most primitive electronic device enables one to amplify sounds to the level that leads to irreversible damage in hearing as well as breaking the rhythm of the internal processes. Furthermore, modern equipment makes it possible to simultaneously extend this influence to a very large audience. In the middle of the 20th century, many countries introduced health and protection regulations limiting the volume of music, probably as a reaction to the new reality of life. A range of allowable volume was designated, which amounted to 90 decibels. In addition, it was established that the uncontrolled use of music by media and certain groups can have a negative impact on humans, especially on young people, exciting them, causing aggression and the urge for destruction.

Music is not just present in our lives — it also shows the hidden processes in us that we can either organize into a coherent picture or let go into a free uncontrollable float. He who has ears to hear, let him hear.

Polina Maratova, Journalist
City of Novosibirsk, Russia
Newspaper "Thoughts and Health," #7, 2009

Everything that exists is music

Why does a person need music?

No one doubts that a child should be taught to read, count, and write. Today, foreign languages are taught from as early as kindergarten. However, when it comes to talking about studying the languages of various kinds of arts, the question immediately arises: What for? Really, what for? Is it really necessary for everyone to understand, for example, the language of music?

Why do people need music? I have asked students, school children, and adults this question. Responses are arranged in the following order: Music is needed for entertainment or to change the mood. Some people note the therapeutic function of music. There are no answers about the main spiritual impact of music. At a music lesson in school one third-grader was asked: "Why don't you sing with others?" He answered: "Who needs this kind of music? Nobody pays for it." Eighth-graders talk about serious music: "Of course, people need serious music, but only those who understand it, who love to listen to it. It is not the music we like though."

In connection with the rapid development of technology and the economic crisis in the late 20th century, it is becoming more and more difficult to explain to people who have a rational way of thinking, the necessity of aesthetic education. This article is the result of the search for answers to the question why music is needed, and this is the analysis and the synthesis of the theoretical and practical research on the topic.

The technological approach to education destroys the emotional and value spheres of an individual. A primitive emotional sphere, along with spiritual inertia, gradually gives rise to cruelty and indifference in the human, limiting the range of joy. Art, which is designed to develop and expand the spiritual elements of man, becomes necessary only as entertainment and is put on a par with a spectacle.

V. Ashkenazi, a pianist and a conductor, was asked by a correspondent of the "Arguments and Facts" newspaper, "If it looked like mass culture was completely replacing classical music." His answer was, "I think these fears have a sufficient basis. As history shows, the majority of people have always preferred to take an easier way, including in relation to art. It is much easier to listen to pop stars because the process of perception of this music does not require any efforts, either mental or spiritual. This music also affects only the most primitive emotions. This culture is for lazy people; we call it a 'down market...' (Newspaper "Arguments and Facts," #47, 2002, page 16).

Through the development of media — TV, radio, audio, video — the entertainment industry is produced and designed for the undemanding tastes of Philistines. When the culture is put on a conveyor belt, then economic rather than cultural factors inevitably come to the forefront. Those who stand at the head of the commercial entertainment market are concerned only about money. A process for the forcible propagation of vulgarity and bad taste is taking place. D. Kabalevsky wrote about epidemic vulgarity. Songs come and go, are forgotten. But their traces remain in the soul, similar to the traces of smallpox left on the face. These epidemics arise because good taste is not brought up, so there is no immunity to bad, vulgar taste.

How music affects a human

The intensification of popular music in everyday life, along with the appearance of powerful audio equipment, leaves modern scientists concerned about the negative effects of music on people. Musicians as well as psychologists, physiologists, biologists, physicists, and geneticists (among many others) are engaged in research in this area because sound, which is the basis for the art of music, has physical parameters: rhythm, frequency, and volume. The analysis of numerous sources leads to the following conclusions.

Rhythm. The impact of rhythm was known since ancient times. The rhythm of the shamanic drum was intended to have a certain impact on the surrounding people. In the last century executions were carried out in open areas accompanied by the loud, hard, monotonous rhythm of the drums to cause fear. Mysteries in honor of the Phrygian goddess Cybele were held with the deafening drumbeats that led priests to self-castration and other forms of self-torture. Bacchantes also brought themselves into a frenzy by the rumble of the drum during festivals in honor of Dionysus.

With a rhythm of 1.5 beats per second accompanied by powerful super frequencies (15-30Hz), a person experiences ecstasy; and at 2 beats per second and the same frequencies, he enters a narcotic state.

In the mid-1960s, pop groups appeared in America that considered themselves "acid-rock" bands. The writing and performing of this kind of music required the use of drugs. Since the 1990s, "acid" or "drive" styles of music were meant for dancing. The basis of this direction is a rhythm tempo with three divisions: 120, 150, and 300 beats per minute.

In nature everything is subject to rhythm. The human body is designed so that it adopts the rhythms dictated by the external environment. Musical rhythm can influence the heart rate and adjust the breathing rhythm. If a person is exposed to a rhythm that is unusual for him, he will feel discomfort, irritation, and aggression. Continued exposure to this rhythm can lead to diseases.

Now imagine "acidic" disco. Music (if it can be called music) is playing for several hours without a break. The rhythm is intensifying; the signals are coming into the brain continuously. There are mainly adolescents from 13 to 20 years old in the hall.

Comments are superfluous.

Frequency. Humans perceive frequencies ranging from 15 - 16 Hz to 20000 - 22000 Hz. The human ear does not perceive frequencies above 22000 Hz, which is ultrasound; however, one can feel the influence of ultrasound. Below this is infrasound, which is also unperceivable to the ear yet still influences the entire body. The best range of perception lies within 800-2000 Hz, whereas frequencies below 50 and above 10000 Hz are not recommended. The natural frequency of the eardrum is 1000 Hz.

Uncontrolled exposure to ultrasound is dangerous, causing damage to internal organs, bleeding, swelling, inflammation, and arthritis. Even ordinary acoustic guitars in the long run may emit ultrasound. When a person is exposed to ultrasound, biochemical reactions similar to a morphine injection occur in the brain.

Infrasound affects the central nervous system. The operating frequency of the brain is about 8 Hz. Infrasound of the same frequency sooner or later causes a response in the nerve cells. This "game" of frequencies accelerates the heartbeat and increases the amount of adrenaline in the blood, causing artificial excitement.

Exposure to low frequencies in combination with light flashes at a frequency of 6-8 Hz deprives a human of deep perception. Light flashes with a frequency of 25 Hz coincide with the frequency of bio waves in the brain, and a person can lose control of his behavior.

Volume. The maximum threshold of sound intensity for a person is the range of 120-130 decibels (causing pain in the ears). For comparison, Niagara Falls has a rating of 90-100 dB and a jet engine has a rating of 120-140 dB. The sound at a pop or rock concert reaches 106-108 dB in the center of the hall and 120 dB near the scene.

Each of these three parameters by itself can have an adverse effect on the body. However, irreversible processes occur in the body with the combination of volume, frequency, and rhythm, such as:

• Secretion of stress hormones that destroy some information in the brain, resulting in the degradation of an individual

• Resonance of the cellular structures of the body, resulting in a state that is similar to the use of drugs and alcohol

• Interruption of the pulse of the human heart and breaking the coordination of the nervous system and endocrine glands

• Cavitation effect (the water molecules in the tissue are heated, the water begins to break the surrounding living matter)

• Damage to internal organs, hemorrhage, edema, arthritis

• Negative effects on the central nervous system

We live in a world of energies, a world of sound. Sound is energy, and like any energy, sound can create and it can also destroy. Unfortunately, our consciousness lags behind technological development. We often do not realize the devastating impact of sound or noise. Western doctors were first to be alarmed about the narcotic effects of rock and pop music as an exaggeration of all three of the aforementioned parameters of sound was the basis precisely of rock and pop music. This led to the emergence of a new concept: music narcotism (narcomania).

Narcomania (from the Greek "narke," dormancy, and "mania," infatuation) is a disease that occurs as a result of the use of drugs that cause euphoria in small doses and stunning or narcotic sleep at high doses. It is characterized by compulsive drug use, the tendency to increase the doses consumed, and the formation of withdrawal syndrome along with mental and physical dependence. Personality changes in the addict increase as the disease progresses. When a teenager repeatedly listens to rock and pop music, he gets used to it and it becomes a necessary background. He wants to listen to it again and again. Listening to this type of music for a long time dulls the sensitivity. A desire to increase the volume appears. From the confession of a girl: "I don't feel well at the concerts of classical music; I run home and turn on the stereo with my music (rock). Then I recover gradually."

The results of a recent study on this problem performed by Doctor of Psychological Sciences A.

Popov, show that if a repetitive listener of rock-pop does not listen to such music for only 3 to 4 days after the regular period, his fingers start trembling at about the same pace as that of an alcoholic.<...>

Everything that exists is music. Man is music. Therefore music is life. We are talking, of course, about harmonious music. There is reason to wonder whether our troubles stem from the fact that we have forsaken harmonious music.

Music yields the palm only to Love, but Love is also Music.

N. Zheleschikova, PhD
Musician, psychologist, and teacher
City of Magnitogorsk, Russia

References:

1. Cosmogony. Plotinus.

2. I got caught...by the guitar. Interview of K. Phil with O. Vanilov, Ph.D. "Live Sound" magazine, #7, 1996, page 11.

Sound, rhythm, music and their influence on humans

Music is a current of energy. It has control over the emotions, the mind, and the disposition. Music is the power that can be used for good or for evil. It is a controlling factor of civilization and its trends. Music that distorts the harmony of sound and rhythm of life itself — rock music, jazz, voodoo rhythms, blues — slowly but inevitably destroys a person: his psyche, morality, soul, mind, feelings, and body.

The world is filled with sounds

We live in a world filled with sounds — audible and inaudible, quiet and loud, chaotic and orderly, soothing and irritating — healing and undermining health.

Since ancient times, people have used sound to get information about the world around them, to communicate with each other.

A baby still in the womb of the mother listens to her heartbeat, hears her voice and music, and makes his own muffled sounds.

Sound is the result of the vibrational motion of particles and objects: from the smallest, such as atoms and electrons to those significantly larger, such as planets.

It is a universal, powerful, invisible force capable of causing both favorable changes (joy, inspiration, healing, relaxation, pacification) and destructive ones (irritation, disorientation, oppression, devastation, disease, and even death).

Musical Sounds

Musical sounds are distinguished from other sounds because their frequencies are interconnected by certain proportions (harmonics). The same proportions can be observed in a variety of natural phenomena from the development of cells and plants to the motion of planets around the Sun. In the man-made world they can be noticed in architecture, art, and mathematics.

The sounds that form a piece of music are subject to a certain rhythm.

Known rhythms — 4/4, 2/4, 3/4, 6/8 — directly correspond to the rhythms of processes in human life.

Why does music have a strong impact on a person?

A person can be compared to a very complex, unique, and finely-tuned musical instrument. Every atom, molecule, cell, tissue, and organ of the body constantly emits frequencies of physical, emotional, mental, and spiritual life.

The structure of tissues and human organs correspond to different frequencies of musical sounds, and the rhythms of the vital processes of the body correspond to different musical rhythms. This leads to the conclusion that music, according to the principle of acoustic resonance, has a very deep and multilateral impact on virtually all functions in the human body (circulation, digestion, respiration, internal secretion, activities of the nervous system and brain, etc.) as well as the emotions, desires, and feelings.

When sound waves penetrate the human body, sympathetic oscillations arise in the cells. The high water content in the tissues helps to transmit sound. The overall mechanical effect in this case can be compared with a deep massage at the atomic and molecular levels.

We can see, then, that music affects the body in two distinct ways: directly, as the effect of sound upon the cells and organs and indirectly, by affecting the emotions, which then in turn influence numerous bodily processes.

The moral beginning in music

Music is a universal human language. It can bypass the logical and analytical filters of consciousness and establish direct contact with heartfelt feelings from the depth of the soul, memory, and imagination. Therefore, respect for life and a sense of responsibility are prerequisites for composing, performing, and using music.

In ancient Greece and Rome, music based on a harmonious foundation was carefully selected to preserve health, purity, and strong character. Pythagoras, Plato, and Aristotle considered music indispensable to the health of the soul, morality, and the flowering of culture.

What kind of music makes us better?

Music in which sounds, rhythm, and musical drawing are subject to the laws of harmony, has a beneficial effect on human health and development: it harmonizes the world of feelings, heals the body, fills with energy and strength; gives food to the soul — spiritual impressions; affects the intellect and brain, improving memory and speeding up the learning process as well as prolonging life.

An example of such music is classical music.

Great composers always felt the connection between music and the physical, moral, and spiritual health of a person. Handel often said that he did not want to entertain listeners with his music; he wanted "to make them better people."

Another example of music that has powerful harmonizing action and great healing power are ancient mantras, chanting, and bhajans. They are a living miraculous legacy for us and for future generations.

Music that has a beneficial effect on the human soul (its development, peace, harmony, liberation) is true folk music.

The impact of perverted sounds and rhythms on a person

Sound and rhythm are fundamental concepts and the basis of the universe.

The order and development of living systems correspond to the exact mathematical formulas of rhythm.

The classical rhythms: 4/4, 2/4, 3/4, and 6/8 correspond to these formulas. Musical styles that use these rhythms contribute to life processes, to the restoration of order and to development.

Works of music that pervert sound or distort these rhythms (distorted music) gradually destroy "the tuning" of the subtle and complex "instrument" that is a person, bringing him closer to spiritual (degradation) and physical death.

The initial impact of such music is perceived as violence and distortion. As the subtle and precise "tuning" of the human body to LIFE and DEVELOP-

MENT breaks down under the influence of this music, a person loses the distinction between good and bad and ceases to resist it, acquiring a bad habit. The pleasure that he receives from this music does not elevate the human consciousness but plunges him into the abyss of animal feelings and passions, aggression, malice, nihilism, drugs, alcohol, nicotine, irresponsible sexual relations, killing unborn children.

The result of the impact of rock music on a person is complete physical and spiritual devastation. For rock stars it becomes possible to exist on the energy of their victims — fans who applaud, cheer, scream, and allow their chakras to be depleted.

The influence of music on the chakras

The entire creation is based upon the mathematical formula of rhythm.

Music accompanies the flow of energy everywhere in the cosmos, in the very cells of life. It is truly the soundless sound that we hear only when we are in tune with its frequency. It has control over the emotions, the mind, and the disposition. According to the proportions, it can be soothing, invigorating, ennobling, vulgarizing, or philosophical.

In the book "The Secret Power of Music," David Tame states: "There is scarcely a single function of the body which cannot be affected by musical

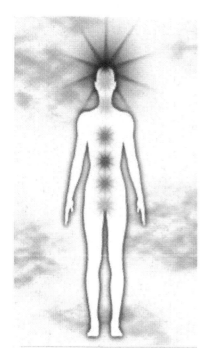

tones... Investigation has shown that music affects digestion, internal secretion, circulation, nutrition and respiration... Music affects the body in two distinct ways: directly, as the effect of sound upon the cells and organs and indirectly, by affecting the emotions, which then in turn influence numerous bodily processes."

Music is a controlling factor of civilization and its trends. Following his teacher Plato, Aristotle said: "The introduction of a new kind of music should be shunned as imperiling the whole state, since new styles of music can never be brought without affecting the most important political institutions."

The perversion of music and rhythm was originally manifested in the **voodoo** beats. Rhythms of voodoo are used in witchcraft and black magic; they cause fear and anxiety, superstition and hatred, death to unexplained causes. This music, injected into the culture of Africa, led to the enslavement of the sons and daughters of Africa by the black magicians.

Jazz was the adaptation of the voodoo beats. Starting in 1835, the Blacks would gather in Congo

Square in New Orleans, and dance, and sing, and perform acts of voodoo. Eventually, these gatherings were disbanded by authorities, but in 1885, Charles Buddy Bolton picked up the spirit of these people and started playing this music in a new way. About 10 years after his new music, Buddy developed a severe mental illness, was committed to a stay in the hospital and died 20 years later. This was the effect of the destruction of jazz upon the temple of the soul.

Jazz became the music of whore houses. Then it became accepted by the public in dance halls and saloons. The resistance to jazz was strong for a while, but nevertheless, this attitude gradually changed, and it became accepted as the way of life.

Jazz is a perversion of **the crown chakra**, taking the wisdom of the Father. Jazz has a jagged pattern, which causes the descent of energy from the crown to the lower chakras. The hypnotic effect upon the dancers and the spectators is the entire point of jazz. It becomes ceremonial music and it affects the rate of the heartbeat. It has a subtle but insistent influence upon both the mind and emotions. It renders an individual out of control of reality because he has literally lost the Mind of God. On first contact with this music, it is violent to the soul, but as it becomes part of our culture, we become accustomed to it, as with all addictions, whether they are alcohol, nicotine, drugs, sugar, or whatever.

Moving to **the heart chakra**, we find that the perfect sound, the rhythm and the tempo of the heart, is found in the waltz. The three-quarter time is the time of the heartbeat of God. In the action of the waltz, there is the balance of the Tai Chi, the ascent of the flow of energy in the four lower bodies. It creates an upward spiral of Light.

By and by, jazz began to pervert the waltz beat. We had the tango and foxtrot and all forms of dance which actually were the perversion of the original three-quarter time.

If we listen to music long enough, our cells and our temples become accustomed to it, and we begin to prefer it. <...>

Within a decade, **rock and roll**, rebellion, sexual liberty, protest, and dope became the mark of a hippy style of life for a large part of the youth. All of this began with music. Jerry Rubin wrote in his book: "Rock and roll marked the beginning of the revolution. We see that sex, rock and roll and dope are a part of the plot to take over America and other countries. When combined, youth, music, sex, drugs, and rebellion with treason, that's a combination hard to beat."

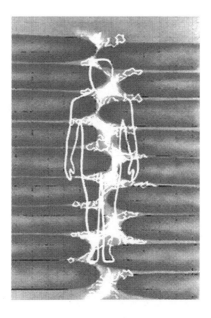

This figure depicts the result of the destructive impact of rock music. This is the aura of a person after listening to "Come Together" performed by the Beatles. What we see here first is the absence of an aura. There is no halo of light around the soul, the chakras, and four lower bodies.

We can also see the process of destruction of the chakras and the release of light from the chakras to the astral plane, where this light is picked up by the hordes of darkness.

"The Beatles" are mainly responsible for introducing drugs, witchcraft, and sex into music, making people believe they are following the course to freedom — their music shocks the heart. The techniques used in this music are the basics to hypnotism and witchcraft through beat and rhythm.

We have this kind of music as background noise in public places. Our food is charged with this death spiral. Everything that we buy, everything that we wear is permeated with these sounds.

The connections of rock to Satanism and voodoo are clear.

"Rolling Stones," the world's greatest rock band, produced an album "Goat Head's Soup." The goat is the symbol of Mendes; the inverted five-pointed star is the symbol of the satanic culture. Part of this album was recorded at a voodoo ritual. Their second album "Sabbath, Bloody Sabbath" actually showed a new satanic mass.

Without rock music the work of the satanic church would have no support in the United States. It was through music and music alone that thousands of people have been drawn into an absolute rebellion against God.

Rock stars are idols of our youth. Rock has become a pagan religion that worships guitar-holding priests and follows all their preaching: using drugs, having sex, and rebelling.

Where do we go then in the music of the future? This presents to us an immense challenge. It is a challenge for all of us to call for the music of the spheres to maintain inner harmony. The sources that were tapped by the great composers of the centuries remain sources of vast expressions of music that can come forward.

What should we do if our children listen to rock music? This is what the psychologist Ph.D. Marilyn C. Barrick advises:

"Your teenagers are doing what teens do, separating out to become their own person, testing the limits, spreading their wings, and trying to fit in with friends.

"Discuss with the family what kind of music stirs and strengthens you, what your favorite songs mean to you. Ask your children what they think might be the effect of negative lyrics and jagged rhythms on one's thoughts, feelings, values, or spirituality. What do they believe writers and musicians hope to accomplish by writing, playing, and singing that kind of music? Listen respectfully, nonjudgmentally, and openheartedly to your children's point of view. Their choice of music is a clue to their inner world, their joys and hopes, fears and anxieties. Encourage your children to share their thoughts and feelings. And remember you have a parental right and responsibility to set limits. Just do so with a lot of love and understanding."

Based on the article of Macrobiotic Center
http://www.macrobios.ru/?p=reviews&row_id=15

References:

1. Elizabeth Clare Prophet. Sound, rhythm and music and their influence on souls and energy current in chakras. Lecture. Summit Lighthouse. 1977.

2. Elizabeth Clare Prophet. Nurturing Your Baby's Soul. Longfello. 2001.

3. Elizabeth Clare Prophet. The Science of Rhythm for the Mastery of the Sacred Energies of Life. Lecture. Summit Lighthouse. 1977.

4. David Tame. The Secret Power of Music. Turnstone Press, Ltd., 1984.

5. Olivia Dewhurst Maddock. The Book of Sound Therapy. Cronpress. 1998.

6. Marilyn C. Barrick, Ph.D. A Spiritual Approach to Parenting. Summit University Press. 2004.

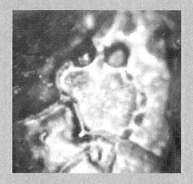

Ordinary water

Spring water

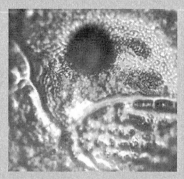

Water from polluted
reservoir

Antarctic ice

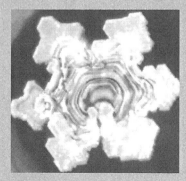

Mozart's Symphony № 40

Beethoven's Pastoral
Symphony

Rock music destroys everything

Thanks to the research of Japanese scientist Masaru Emoto, we can get an objective picture of the powerful ability of music to transform the world and energy, taking as an example its impact on water.

Water is a very familiar yet quite an extraordinary substance. The internal structure of water is a hierarchy of equilateral volumetric structures, which are based on a crystal like "quantum of water," which consists of 57 molecules. This energetically stable structure can be destroyed physically only in a solution with a high concentration of alcohol or similar solvent.

"Water Quanta," when grouping, can form a second order structure in the form of hexagons of 912 water molecules.

The structure of water makes a copy of the energetic informational field in which it is located.

Biologically active and the most suitable for living organisms, "healthy water" corresponds to a hexagonal crystal structure with well-formed connections.

Masaru Emoto's experiments on the effects of different music on water show that different hexagonal crystalline structures are formed in ordinary water as a result of exposure to certain kinds of music.

 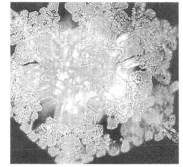

Kawachi folk dance   HADO healing music

A distinctive feature of these pieces of music is the matching of their musical pattern, rhythm, and sound to the laws of harmony — structural laws and rhythms of developmental processes that are inherent in the fundamental order of Life in all its manifestations.

This is classical music, true folk music, as well as ancient chants, true patriotic songs, and oriental mantras.

Attuning us to the harmony of Life, this music can heal body and soul, as well as energize and replenish the creative activity.

If you prefer this kind of music, your mind and your inner world are attuned to harmony, creativity, health, and development.

When regular water is exposed to other types of music, the crystal structure is not formed and the previously well-formed crystal structure of the water breaks down.

This destructive action is characteristic of distorted music: all types of rock music, jazz, voodoo, tango, foxtrot, blues, and "soul," which distort the harmony of rhythm and sound inherent to human life, nature, and the universe; upset vital

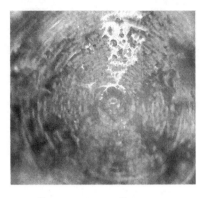

"Heavy rock" music

structures and processes and devastate their energy, despite the simultaneous short-term impression of physical and emotional excitement and pleasure (turning later into a negative state of consciousness).

If you like this kind of music and you allow yourself to be where it is playing, your physical and mental health is at risk, as it slowly but inevitably destroys the vital links in the world and man, bringing his psychology, morals, soul, mind, feelings, and body into the process of degradation.

Many people believe that liking one kind of music and rejecting another kind is a matter of taste. However, this "taste" is formed on the principle of energy — the informational similarity of music to a person's consciousness, his aspirations, and his inner world.

If we are inwardly directed to harmony, peace, and love for all living beings, we perceive the distorted music as violence, discord, cacophony, and chaos.

If a person's consciousness is focused on itself, limited by mind installations, material interests, and the desire for pleasures, then he will not be able to hear the vital richness of classical music, its life-giving rewards graciously descending to us from the spheres of Light and Harmony, satisfying our extreme need and hunger for them.

Source: "Rock music destroys everything"
Booklet of the youth committee of
the organization "Summit Lighthouse,"
City of Zheleznogorsk, Russia

Music is a weapon!

The destruction of any state begins
with the destruction of its music,
People who do not have pure and
light music are doomed to extinction.
Confucius

Music is the subtlest and yet most powerful sphere of culture. It can be a powerful tool for perfection and creation or for destruction!

The resourceful Odysseus, King of Ithaka, one day while sailing the seas, came to an island where the sirens — half women, half birds — lived. They lured sailors going by with their sweet singing and put them to cruel death. None of the sailors could resist the magical, alluring power of their singing. The entire island was strewn with the bones of people torn to pieces by them. To successfully pass the island, Odysseus closed up the rowers' ears with soft wax so that they did not hear the sirens' baneful singing; he also ordered his men to tie him to the mast. Only when the island of sirens was left far behind, fellow travelers of Odysseus took the wax out of their ears and untied him from the mast.

The ancient Greek manuscripts read: "Musical education is the most powerful weapon, because rhythm and harmony penetrate the innermost depths of the human soul."

<...>

Music can extend or shorten life! Traditional healers and shamans know that with the help of rhythm, you can speed up or slow down the heart rate. Some African tribes were known for executing criminals by means of drumming. Certain disco-club rhythms destroy the work of the heart to such an extent, that one can become a sick old person in two years!

In ancient times people understood: violation of the laws of musical harmony deforms the soul and destroys the human body, its internal structure and relations with the outer world. In ancient China, a person who composed inharmonious music could be executed!

There are a number of styles, trends, and directions in music that are dangerous to man. Aggressive, protesting-destructive, darkly depressing, stupefying-intoxicating in their nature, they distort the meaning of musical-semantic harmonies, replacing them with powerful effects and the flow of the negative impact on the audience.

An intelligent person, even without understanding the intricacies of music and lyrics, is usually able to distinguish harmful, dangerous music by his own negative impressions. Despite the fact that the perception of music is individual, it is as simple as distinguishing black from white, good from evil, sadness from joy, nice from mean.

At the present time, there are a great number of musical styles that are sometimes closely intertwined with each other and, when combined, create new ones. Therefore, it is hardly worth dividing music into "useful," "neutral," and "harmful" according to the style. There are certain signs of dangerous combinations of sounds, sound settings, methods of performing, meaning and imaging, which will be mentioned below. This knowledge will help you to make your choice.

Evil "rock" and black "rap"

The emergence of rock music as protest music in the 1950's was marked by suicide outbreaks and psychogenic epidemic, destroying the moral barriers that were designed to deter the brute and base inclinations of man. It affected particularly the intimate spheres of life. The beginning of the rock epidemic was also the beginning of the drug epidemic and the so-called sexual revolution. It put an end to the suppression of the carnal instincts and other moral prohibitions. Everything was allowed!

In the 1980's there appeared punk rock (in England the word "punk" originally referred to a prostitute of both sexes). The philosophy and purpose of punk rock was to direct the audience to suicide, collective violence, and systematic crimes. The supreme "achievement" of a punk was inflicting bloody wounds to somebody by a razor blade, sewn into the punk's jeans or shirt, and beating the wounded with a bracelet covered with thorns and nails.

The American press wrote about a 14-year-old girl from California, who murdered her own mother. She stabbed her with a knife a number of times. At the trial, it was established that at the time of the crime the girl had been in a state of extreme nervous excitement after having listened to music in the style of "hard rock."

How does rock music achieve a negative influence on man? All the techniques of rock music are taken from ancient and modern secret societies and fraternities of black magic. The rhythm, the frequency of the alternation between light and dark, as well as the jumble of sounds, are aimed at the destruction of the human being, at forcible change, and at breaking his self-defense mechanisms, self-preservation instinct, and moral principles. The rhythm acquires narcotic properties. For example, if the rhythm is equal to 1.5 beats per second and accompanied by a strong pressure of ultralow frequencies (15-30 Hz), it can cause a person to experience ecstasy. When the rhythm is equal to two beats per second at the same frequencies, the listener falls into a dancing trance, which is similar to a narcotic state.

There were cases where an overflow of high or low frequencies seriously injured the brain. At rock concerts there were also numerous sound contusions, sound burns, loss of hearing and memory. Volume and frequency reached such a destructive force that in 1979, a wooden bridge collapsed during a concert by Paul McCartney in Venice, and the group "Pink Floyd" managed to destroy a bridge in Scotland. Another "achievement" to which there was a testimony, belonged to the same group: Sound-stunned fish surfaced in a nearby lake during one of their outdoor concerts.

Both rhythm and frequency lead to addiction to them: a person acquires the need for still higher frequencies, approaching ultrasound. This is fraught with a fatal outcome (cases of death have been recorded by American doctors).

A person also develops a need for intensified rhythm. "The Beatles" played at a power level of 500-600 watts. By the end of the 1960's, "The Doors" reached 1000 watts. Several years later, 20-30 thousand watts became the norm. AC/DC already performed at a level of 70 thousand watts. This is also not the limit. Is it a lot or a little? This is quite a lot, because even a hundred watts in a small concert hall can affect a person's ability to think and analyze.

Immersion into a sound "bag" affects the ability to orientate oneself and to make one's own decisions. Russian scientists recorded the following: After 10 minutes of listening to heavy rock, seventh-graders forgot the multiplication table for some time. Japanese journalists randomly asked the audience in the largest rock concert halls of Tokyo just three simple questions: "What is your name? Where are you? What year is it now?" None of the respondents answered the questions. According to the German professor B. Rauch, this kind of music caused the release of so-called stress hormones that erased part of the information in the brain. A person did not simply forget something that had happened to him or something that he had studied. He became mentally degraded. Not long ago, Swiss doctors proved that after a rock concert, people's orientation and response to stimulus became three to five times worse than usual.

Aggressive rock took a full set of black magic rituals, incantations, and spells in order to reproduce as accurately as possible the rhythms that lead the audience to ecstatic experience. Rhythm strongly excites all the emotional, physical, and physiological pulsations causing a strong stimulation of the nervous system and paralysis of the thought process. The intensity of sound reaches 120 dB, while the human ear is tuned to an average intensity of 55 dB. The impact of the extremely loud noises on the human body is destructive; this kind of music is called by experts "killer-music" or "sound-poison." This is a decisive assault on the entire human personality. The exciting pulsations of the rhythm are added to the bewitching effect of the irritating noise, which by its nature leads to a nervous overstrain. It creates a high voltage environment to give vent to strong passions, entailing their natural satisfaction. Drums, guitars, trumpets, electronic synthesizers, light effects, shrill cries, body movements — everything is bursting with all its fierce force and permeates the sensitive human body.

The acceleration of the alternation of footlights and darkness leads to a significant weakening of orientation, along with reducing the speed of the reflexes. At a certain speed, flashes of light begin to interact with the brain's alpha waves, which control the ability to concentrate. With a further increase in frequency, there is a complete loss of control.

The entire technical arsenal of heavy rock aims to manipulate, playing man like a musical instrument. This music is able to totally change the individual characteristics of a person because it simultaneously affects his motor, emotional, and sexual centers. That is, the effect of this music applies to all dimensions of the human personality: physiological, psychological, psycho-emotional, and spiritual.

Physiological disorders include: a change in pulse and respiration; changes in the spinal cord function (the autonomic nervous system associated with the unconscious sphere of the individual); changes in vision, attention, hearing, blood sugar; and an increase in secretion of the endocrine glands. Bob Larsen's team of American doctors clearly state: "Low frequency oscillations created by the force of bass guitar, to which the repetitive action of rhythm is added, have a significant impact on the state of the cerebrospinal fluid. This fluid, in its turn, directly affects the gland regulating secretion of hormones as well as substantially changing the blood insulin level. As a result, the balance of sexual and adrenal hormones is broken so that various functions of control of moral inhibition fall below the threshold of tolerance or become entirely neutralized."

If one exposes himself for a long time to the influence of rock music, then it is impossible not to get deep psycho-emotional traumas. As a result, there is a loss of control over one's ability to concentrate, significantly weakening control over the mental activity and will; unbridled impulses lead to destruction, vandalism, and rebellion, especially at large gatherings.

The capacity for sound reasoning is heavily affected — it turns out to be strongly blunted and sometimes even completely neutralized. It is in this state of mental and moral confusion that a green light is given to the most savage, previously-restrained passions, such as hatred, anger, jealousy, vindictiveness, and cruelty. All this taken together means that the barriers of morality are breaking down as well as the automatic reflexes and mechanisms of natural protection disappearing. All this is aimed at capturing a person with the subconscious messages of some performer.

A subconscious message is the information that is perceived by a person beyond the threshold of his consciousness — that is, by his subconscious. Such messages cannot be detected using the faculties of consciousness. It has been established that only one-seventh of the information is perceived by consciousness, and six-sevenths of it are perceived by the subconscious. Subliminal messages avoid hearing, sight, and other external senses and penetrate into the very depth of the subconscious. In case of continuous exposure of the brain to a subconscious sound signal for a long period of time, a biochemical reaction occurs in it, similar to that of a morphine injection. When a person is in a narcotic trance, subliminal messages turn into programs that are mandatory for execution. This is total collective obfuscation and zombification.

The main danger is that a defenseless audience is completely unaware that it is experiencing this deepest intrusion into the holy of holies of its being — the realm of consciousness, the subconscious, and the superconscious. Messages caught in the subconscious area are deciphered and reconstructed to be transmitted through memory to the conscious "I," passing through barriers and thresholds associated with the accumulated moral experience, bypassing individual and collective archetypes.

Subliminal messages can carry the following course of actions:

1) All kinds of perversions

2) Calls for rebellion against the established order

3) Inducement to suicide

4) Incitement to violence and murder

5) Ordaining to evil and Satan

For subtler and less noticeable transmission of subliminal messages, phrases are inserted in reverse — that is, in such a way that they become legible only when the recording is played backwards. The conducted research shows that the subconscious can catch the phrase written backwards and decipher the message expressed, it would seem, in an apparently unknown language to the audience. Information designed for the perception of consciousness and the subconscious sometimes contains, in addition to the propaganda of violence, the glorification of hellish forces. In the song  "Anthem" by the rock band "Rush," these are the lyrics: "Oh, Satan, you are the one who is shining… wall of Satan, I know it is you are the one I love…" Here is an excerpt from the song "God of Thunder" by the rock band "Kiss": "I was raised by the demons. Trained to reign as the one. I am the lord of the wastelands, a modern-day man of steel. I gather darkness to please me, and I command you to kneel before the god of thunder and rock & roll." The word "Kiss" itself is an acronym for "Knights in Satan's Service." In witch language "knights" are messengers who take part in the cult of Satan. This band seeks, above all, to praise violence, sadomasochism, and all the symbolisms of evil and unrestrained perversions. This band not only uses subliminal messages, but also systematically composes songs that glorify Satan and salute the onset of his world domination.

The rock band AC/DC praises the bells of hell: "I am a rolling thunder, a pouring rain, I'm comin' on like a hurricane, my lightning's flashing across the sky. You're only young, but you're gonna die. I won't take no prisoners, won't spare no lives, nobody is putting up a fight. I got my bell, I'm gonna take you to hell. I'm gonna get you, Satan get you. Hell's bells, yeah, hell's bells" (from the song "Hell's Bells"). This rock band mainly focuses on the glorification of Satan and hell and calls for devotion to Satan in order to find happiness in hell for eternity. This band is the most destructive, perverted, and satanic. The very name AC/DC stands for "Antichrist." They also have the songs "Highway to Hell,"and "Shoot to Thrill."

In the song of punk rock band "Dead Kennedy" entitled "I Kill Children," it says: "I kill children. I love to see them die. I kill children. And make their mammas cry. Crush 'em under my car. I wanna hear them scream. Feed 'em poison candy to spoil their Halloween."

Sometimes aggressive performers arrange bacchanals on stage. Alice Cooper tossed snakes into the auditorium, often feigned the death penalty by hanging himself on stage, played with a cauldron filled with the blood, guts, and giblets of animals, and threw them without warning into the auditorium. Punk bands considered it especially cool to urinate on stage.

The provocative statements of some "stars" amaze people with their cynicism and unhealthy ambitions. Graham Nash states: "Pop music is the medium of communication that determines the personal thought of the one who listens to it. I also imagine that through this music the musicians have a fantastic supremacy. "We can conduct the world. We have at our disposal the necessary strength." Mick Jagger, who calls himself the Lucifer of rock, declares: "We are moving after the minds and so are most of the new groups."

Now think about whether you want to be conducted, controlled, or manipulated? Will you be good in the role of one of the numerous puppets in the hands of musical idols? Is everything right with the heads of those who invite you to the nether world, advise you to kill ruthlessly and to destroy violently? They are convincing, because they want it! They are sincere with you! You can become a dark destructive force controlled by their music!

Scientists researched the connection between young people's addiction to the "heavy metal" style of music and suicidal tendencies. Fans of this style were characterized by less zest for life (especially young men) and a greater frequency of thoughts about suicide (especially young women). Russian psychologist D. Azarov once confessed: "I managed to distinguish a combination of notes, similar for all suicides of rock musicians. When I listened to this musical phrase several times, I felt such a surge of gloomy mood that I myself was ready to climb into the noose. A lot of musical works of our time are created from "killer-sounds"!

Plants and animals prefer harmonious music. If classical music accelerates the growth of wheat, then rock music does the opposite. If, under the influence of classical music, the amount of milk increases in nursing mothers and mammals, then under the influence of rock music it drops sharply. Dolphins enjoy listening to classical music, especially Bach. Hearing classical works, sharks calm down and gather from all over the ocean; plants and flowers quickly spread their leaves and petals under influence of classical music. With the sounds of heavy rock, cows lie down and refuse to eat and plants quickly fade.

<...>

Will we succeed in avoiding the harmful aggressive influence of songs if we only listen to the instrumental music in them or listen to songs in an unfamiliar language? The answer is unequivocal: Whether you listen to the lyrics or not, the music itself is the bearer of certain energies, emotions, and thoughts!

Music in the rhythm "Delta"

The rhythm of music with a frequency of about 130-150 beats per minute falls into the category of "shamanic frequencies." The beat of the "magic" tambourine was used by shamans of different nationalities for bringing people into a trance and performing witch rituals. This rhythm coincides with the frequency of the delta waves of the brain, observed on the electroencephalogram in a state of sleep, trance, or coma. This is the rhythm of synchronous activity of a large amount of nerve cells modulated in a frequency of two to three Hz, which corresponds to the delta rhythm of the brain.

Music in this rhythm, often playing at clubs and other social venues, under certain conditions can become extremely dangerous. Unlike jazz or classical music, this rhythm is accented, very loud, and almost devoid of variation. At these venues when rhythmic dance and rhythmic flashing of bright light in the darkness are added to the music, together they represent a complete set of psycho-technical methods that cause the domination of the delta rhythm in the brain.

A dancing person immerses his or her brain for several hours into conditions that can cause an artificial, minor epileptic fit or provoke a stuck-up type of thinking with any obsession, including suicide. Moreover, the numerous hours of such "shamanistic" trance cause the effect of habituation and changes in the structure of the brain.

The monotonous pulsations of bass in the rhythm of "delta," inherent in club disco techno-music, change the rhythm of brain activity. The listener must integrate into the delta rhythms, synchronize with them, and eventually fall into some kind of trance. A number of specialists involved in Chinese medicine state that such music disrupts the flow of energy that connects us to past and future lives.

Italian scientists conducted studies on the influence of music in the rhythm of delta on physiology.

In their opinion music in the style of "house" contributes to the temporary appearance of impotence. These findings suggest that a strongly expressed rhythm and almost complete absence of melody extinguish sexual desires.

* * *

One can say, "If such music exists then someone needs it." Yes, our diverse world consists of perfection and imperfection. Every person is free to choose what is better for him. However, in order to protect yourself and the world from destruction, you must fill it with beauty!

Only harmonious music makes a man more perfect and the world more beautiful!

Based on the article by Michail Svetov
"Music Energetics. Power and Magic of Sound"
Source: "Global" magazine, Russia.
http://global-project.ru/music_weapon

About music therapy

What is music? Each person will answer this question in his own way. One will say that it is a kind of art, another that it is notes and sounds, and yet a third that it is melody and rhythm. They all are right.

What is sound?

Music is a kind of art in which artistic images are expressed through sounds. Then what are sounds? Sounds are vibrations, waves of a certain frequency, energy of a certain kind. Sounds spread in the air by waves — that is, sound waves are floating from a speaker in all directions. As a result, our ear membranes vibrate, and this way we catch a sound or impulse.

Brain nerve impulses that occur with certain sounds have the same frequency as the sounds themselves. Our brain distinguishes not only the basic tones of sounds but also the overtones of the high frequency.

Each of us is able to distinguish between "good" and "bad" sounds. Sounds in the environment are assessed in part subjectively, but the influence of most of them can be fixed or measured with the help of different devices. We can objectively characterize their impact on our mood, tone, pulse, brain waves, and digestion. It follows from the above that, in particular, the influence of sounds on the body for the most part is beyond our control. If it is undesirable, the only way to resist it is to isolate yourself from the source of the sounds, and this is not always possible. Thus, music affects people and changes the constant vibration of the molecules of the human body.

The influence of music in different spheres of life

Life in a modern, urbanized society is full of physical and emotional stress factors, such as overpopulation, environmental pollution, noise, radiation, poor quality food, various chemical additives, anxiety, loneliness, too much or too little physical activity, and malaise.

Taken separately and collectively, these stressors cause overexertion, which starts to interfere with the free flow of energy in the body, resulting in the body's organs overheating. In addition, there are few "living" places in the concrete jungle in which we live; forests, parks, open spaces, flowing water-streams and rivers are the sources of cool, cleansing energy.

A prolonged overheating causes the organs to contract and solidify. This worsens their activity and causes illness. Music therapy, as one of the means, helps the body to remove all barriers and arrange the blocked energy properly, to direct it to the normal course. This way, we help ourselves, we heal. With music therapy, there is a simultaneous influence of acoustic waves, organized into a musical structure, on the psycho-emotional and spiritual spheres of a person and directly on the surface of the body and internal organs. The main task of healing is to unite the conscious and the unconscious in the physical body with the help of music and singing.

In ancient times music was considered to be of great importance. The Celts had entire schools where bards were trained in the field of studying, composing, and spreading music. They composed song spells, possessing a huge sacral force, curing or causing irreparable harm. Such spells were passed only to the worthy and kept in strict secret.

Pythagoras created the teaching of the music of the spheres and the musical scale, in which every planet corresponds to a certain note; he initiated musical psychotherapy as a means of education and treatment of the soul and body. Plato believed that the best protection of a state is not an army and perfect weapons but simple, modest, sedate, and harmonious music. The Chinese put music in a row with mathematics and astronomy. Avicenna used music for treatment and affirmed the connection between music and pulse.

For the purposes of therapy, music began to be used actively in the 19th and 20Th centuries, first in the West and in America, and then in Russia. The interest of Russian scientists to the problem of the influence of music on the human body manifested itself in a number of studies conducted by V. M. Bekhterev, S. S. Korsakov, I. M. Dogil, I. M. Sechenov, I. R. Tarkhanov, G. P. Shipulin, and others. Studies revealed the beneficial effect of music on various systems of the human body: cardiovascular, respiratory, motor, nervous, as well as normalization of cerebral blood circulation. Very important conclusions were made that positive emotions obtained from contact with art and music had a therapeutic effect on psycho-emotional tension, mobilized reserve forces, and stimulated creativity.

Nowadays there is a revival in Russia in scientific studies researching the impact of music on the human body — music therapy. In Moscow since 2003, the Russian Research Center for Restorative Medicine and Balneology of the Ministry of Health and Social Development has been preparing professionals, under the leadership of S. V. Shushardjan, in the field of music therapy. In St. Petersburg numerous training seminars have been conducted and CDs with healing music recorded at the Scientific Research Institute of Traditional Music Therapy, founded by Rushel Blavo. In this way, many diseases and mental disorders have been treated using music therapy.

Scientists, physicians, and psychologists have identified the impact of various styles of music on the body. So-called "commercial music" such as pop, hip-hop, rock, and heavy rock, is written in low frequencies. Studies have shown that low-frequency sounds have, for the most part, a negative effect on humans. They cause exhaustion and depression or are perceived as threatening — for example, thunder or the rumble of an earthquake, continuous noise, and hard rock. Rock music slows down plant growth.

After a rock concert, the concert goers react three to five times slower than normal to natural stimuli. Listening to rock music causes the release of so-called stress hormones, which erase a large part of the stored information in the brain. The repeated rhythm and low frequency oscillations of the bass guitar strongly influence the state of the cerebrospinal fluid and, as a consequence, the functioning of the glands that regulate the secretions of hormones; the level of insulin in the blood changes significantly; and the main indicators of control of moral inhibition fall below the threshold of tolerance or are completely neutralized.

Under the influence of excessively loud, rhythmic music, the crowd often becomes aggressive. However, in an aggressive environment the body attunes itself to this music, and it becomes the norm for it. In general, while functioning in our usual everyday urban life with its fuss, noise, stress, and negative emotions, we are in the beta-wave range (14-20 Hz).

Higher, more energetic sounds with a clear rhythm and moderate tempo affect us positively, raising the level of energy, both physical and mental, causing joy and lightening the mood. It's here that harmonic overtones come into play. Overtones are subtle, barely audible shades of high frequency accompanying all the sounds around us. Only harmonic overtones can instill liveliness in us and charge us with energy. It is useful to listen to such music in the morning, getting charged with cheerfulness and optimism for the whole day.

When listening to classical, folk, church music, or to the sounds of nature, we calm down, relax, and saturate ourselves with positive energy, emotions, and harmony. After all, the smaller the sound wave is, the more relaxed we are. Classical music is characterized by the rhythm of the body, equal to 60 beats per minute, which leads to a state in the alpha range (8-13 Hz). It is the state of rest and exalted feelings. Such music is useful to listen to after a hard day because it counteracts feelings of fatigue and loss of strength.

When we sleep, meditate, and create (the state of inspiration), we are in the state of theta frequencies (4-7 Hz). With deep meditation and unconsciousness, delta waves are produced (0.5-3 Hz).

Currently, music therapy is used to treat many diseases as well as in psychotherapy, trade, and agriculture. It has been noticed that in the process of music playing and singing, thinking becomes a more active, purposeful activity, and stability of attention are formed in students with mental retardation. Listening to music and rhythmical exercises has beneficial effect on the development of speech function, attentiveness, and motor skills in children with hearing impairment.

Scientists and teachers have noticed that the musical art, when applied in its various combinations (with movements and theatrical activities) in relation to a child with developmental problems, acts as a source of positive experience for the child, gives rise to new creative needs and ways to satisfy them, as well as ensuring the formation of musical culture and correcting deviations in the cognitive, emotional-volitional, and personal spheres, thereby creating conditions for social adaptation.

Classical music heals

Scientists consider the music of J. S. Bach to be the strongest in terms of impact, while the music of W . A. Mozart and L. van Beethoven is considered the second most influential. The music of Bach and Handel, written in the Baroque style, has a relaxing effect, helps to improve memorization and memory, and helps with learning foreign languages and learning poems by heart.

The phenomenon of Mozart's music is explained by the fact that the vibrations of his works coincide with the vibrations of healthy neurons.

Thus, in Holland, milk yields increase when using Mozart's music. Dough rises several times faster and becomes better, softer, and tastier with the music of this outstanding composer. By using the music of Mozart when preparing for exams, students more quickly and successfully absorb and memorize educational material and pass their tests. The music of Mozart and Tchaikovsky contributes to the treatment of Parkinson's and Alzheimer's diseases.

The so-called music of nature is also very useful. The sounds of the sea, sounds of the rain, the voices of dolphins soothe and pacify; the sounds of the forest lower blood pressure and normalize the work of the heart; the singing of birds helps to cope with thoughts and causes a surge of positive emotions.

Scientists have found that birds' singing contributes to the growth and development of plants. In Florida, for example, orange groves are irrigated using music that imitates the singing of birds. Such oranges are not only sweeter but also have 121% more vitamin C than usual.

In India, rice plantations are stimulated through traditional Indian music. Productivity of crops increases by 25-67%.

In Germany, such music is curative and it is sold only in pharmacies. In China, there are discs developed under the names "Liver," "Heart," "Intestines," "Stomach," etc., which contain music beneficial for these organs.

In Canada, string orchestras play in city squares to reduce the number of accidents. It has been noticed that by listening to classical music in the car, drivers reduce the risk of emergency situations by 15 times. Listening to folk and classical music in shuttle buses leads to an improvement in the microclimate in the cabin as well as a drastic decrease in aggression and irritability of passengers.

The therapeutic effect when stroking a cat is achieved thanks to the purring of the pet, the vibration of which has a beneficial effect on our bodies.

Vibrations of ringing bells also have a powerful, healing effect. In the Middle Ages, people used to save themselves from the plague epidemics by ringing church bells. The sound of a bell creates vibrations over 25 kHz, increasing immunity. The medium spectrum of bell sounds (100-120 kHz) increases capillary blood flow and lymph flow; and the low spectrum of bell sounds (40-100 kHz) soothes the psyche. This affects all people, regardless of their faith.

Prayers and appeals to God also cause a certain effect. Most of the prayers are aimed at improving the body — they contribute to cleansing and healing. The phenomenon of the icons, often prayed at, is that the frequent repetition of "encoded messages" (prayers) in front of the same icon allows one to leave certain information on the surface of this icon. A wave aura of a certain frequency is created around such an icon, and it influences a person by itself. Therefore, it is absolutely effective to ask for help from a holy image. Get your own holy images and icons, appeal to them with love and gratitude, and they will serve you as a source of high vibrations and healing.

Scientists and doctors have revealed the influence of classical music on the state of our health.

Relieve pain and emotional stress:

• M. K. Oginski. Polonaise "Farewell to the Fatherland"

• F. Liszt. "Hungarian Rhapsody-1"

• L. van Beethoven. "Fidelio"

• A. I. Khachaturyan. "Masquerade Suite"

• A. Dvorak. "Humoresks"

Remove neuroses, irritability, disappointment, rise over everyday life into higher spheres:

• L. van Beethoven. "Moonlight Sonata"

• J. S. Bach. "Italian Concert", "Cantata №2"

• G. F. Handel's music

Soothe, reduce anxiety and insecurity:

• F. P. Schubert. "Ave Maria"

• F. F. Chopin. Mazurkas and Preludes. Nocturne in G minor

• J. Brahms. "Lullaby"

• J. B. Strauss. Waltzes

• C. Debussy. "Moon Light"

• L. van Beethoven. "Symphony 6, part 2"

Decrease narcotic dependence on alcoholism and nicotine:

• F. P. Schubert. "Ave Maria"

• L. van Beethoven. "Moonlight Sonata"

- G. V. Sviridov. "Snowstorm"
- C. Saint-Saens. "Swan"

Restore normal blood pressure and heart activity, relieve tension in relationships with other people:
- F. F. Chopin. "Nocturne in D Minor"
- F. Mendelssohn. "Wedding March"
- J. S. Bach. "Cantata 21", "Concerto in D Minor for Violin"
- B. Bartok. "Sonata for Piano"
- A. Bruckner. "Mass in A Minor"

Treat insomnia:
- E. H. Grieg. Suite "Per Gynt"
- J. Sibelius. "Sad Waltz"
- R. Schumann. "Dreams"
- P. I. Tchaikovsky. Plays

Relieve gastritis:
- L. van Beethoven. "Sonata №7 for Piano"

Reduces joint pain:
- W. A. Mozart's music

Treat Epilepsy:
- W. A. Mozart's music

Improve eyesight:

- W. A. Mozart's music

Increase mental abilities in children:

- W. A. Mozart's music

Stimulate mental activity:

- L. van Beethoven's music
- J. B. Strauss's music

Treat the syndrome of chronic fatigue:

- E. H. Grieg. "Morning" (from "Per Gynt")
- M. P. Mussorgsky. "Dawn over the Moscow River" (Overture to "Khovanshchina")
- A. A. Alyabyev. Romance "Evening Ringing"

Stimulate the growth of plants:

- G. A. Rossini's music
- Violin Sonatas by J. S. Bach

Increase vitality, improve health, mood, activity, and creative energy:

- P. I. Tchaikovsky. "Sixth Symphony, part № 3"
- F. F. Chopin. "Prelude 1, opus 28"
- F. Liszt. "Hungarian Rhapsody -2"
- L. van Beethoven. Overture to "Edmond"

About the influence of musical Instruments

Harmonious melodies and sounds literally recharge our internal batteries with vital energy. To do this you can simply listen to the performance of certain instruments. You can also use the simplest and closest instrument to you — your own voice!

Here are the results of the study of the impact of musical instruments on the human body:

• **Violin** — heals the soul, helps self-knowledge and has a very beneficial effect on melancholics.

• **Organ** — brings the mind in order, harmonizes the energy flow of the spine, it is a conductor between the cosmos and the Earth.

• **Piano** — affects the kidneys, bladder and cleanses the thyroid glands.

• **Drum** — restores the rhythm of the heart and stimulates the circulatory system.

• **Flute**—- cleans the bronchopulmonary system, heals unhappy love and removes irritation and embitterment.

• **Bayan, accordion** — activates the work of the abdominal cavity.

• **Harp and string instruments** — harmonize the work of the heart, treat hysteria and blood pressure.

• **Saxophone** — activates sexual energy, the sexual system.

• **Clarinet, flute-piccolo** — suppress despondency and improve blood circulation.

• **Contrabass, celo, guitar** — affect the heart and small intestine, treat the kidneys.

• **Tsimbala** — balances the liver.

• **Balalaika** — treats the digestive system.

• **Trumpet** — treats lower back pain.

<...>

Harmonious music is the safest preventative means. It does not cause side effects and negative consequences. It is prescribed to everybody without exception. This is a remedy that is accessible to everyone and will never cause harm. Aspiring towards the beautiful and spiritual is primordial in a person. It is an aspiration for something that can give energy, support, and inspiration. Music allows you to hear yourself as well as to find harmony with nature and surrounding life. Therefore, it is so necessary for each of us to learn the true musical culture.

Elena Luchina
Moscow, Russia

References:

1. B. D. Aranovich. The Healing Power of Music.

2. O. Slaboda. Healing through the Magic of Sounds.

3. D. Campbell. Articles about the Healing Power of Music.

4. H. I. Khan. Mysticism of Sound.

5. Chia Mantec. Six Healing Sounds.

6. S. Shusharjan. Health by Notes.

7. S. Shusharjan. Music Therapy. History and Prospects.

Messages of the Ascended Masters

Words of Wisdom

Volume I

Tatyana N. Mickushina

Messages
of the Ascended
Masters — Words of Wisdom — II

Messages
of the Ascended
Masters — Words of Wisdom — III

Messages
of the Ascended
Masters — Words of Wisdom — IV

Words of Wisdom — V

Quotations about Music from the books "Words of Wisdom"

The series of books "Words of Wisdom" are the messages of the Masters of Wisdom, the Great Teachers of mankind, transmitted through Tatyana N. Mickushina. The books contain a new philosophical and ethical Teaching that reveals the Wisdom of Ancient Knowledge in modern language.

The Teaching was received by T. N. Mickushina in the years from 2005 to 2015, and individual messages still continue to come into the world.

Tatyana N. Mickushina is a well-known public figure, philosopher, and author of more than 60 books. Her books have been translated into 20 languages. They have been published in over 10 countries around the world. You can find more information on the author's site: **sirius-eng.net**

Quotations from the messages, published in this digest, are devoted to music and culture.

From the Editorial Board

"Be able to discriminate in your life the right Divine patterns from the false ones inculcating in you the culture of death and hell.

Banish from your life everything that is not from God, all the lies flowing into your consciousness through the TV screens and computers. Seek and find the right patterns around you. Cultivate them.

It depends on you alone where you will invest your money earned so painfully. Either you will spend it on getting pointless pleasures from life or on providing your children an access to cultural values of the past and the present.

The music of Russian composers and the pictures of Russian painters of the 18th and 19th centuries are rich in those vibrations that can neutralize the vibrations of death implanted into your consciousness while watching TV programs and listening to the music that has spread throughout the territory of Russia recently.

Protect your children from watching TV programs and listening to rock music. ...The benefits from using your modern mass media cannot be compared with the harm unconsciously being done to their souls.

Use every opportunity to be in nature. Spend some time in nature but without having a barbecue and listening to music and commercials on the radio.

Listen to the sounds of nature. Look at the birds, at the trees. Look at the clouds. Listen to the silence..."

From Words of Wisdom Volume 1[2],
March 27, 2005.

"...the world is filled with very low vibrations. And it is very difficult to tune into the Divine harmony amidst the confusion of your world. That is why we really recommend that you to spend as much time as possible in nature and in silence. The rustlings of grasses, the twittering of birds, even the buzzing of insects are the sounds mostly close to our world.

Learn to listen to the voices of nature; learn to contemplate nature and to pass it through yourself. Learn to pass the pictures of nature that surround you through your consciousness.

When you happen to be in silence on the bank of the river or on the sea shore, in the forest or in the field, you are really in the Temple of God. And you should feel an utterly Divine quivering before the care of God about you. He has built the most perfect Temples for you.

Your stay in nature should be akin to visiting a temple. Thank God for every minute of silence when you are staying in His Temple and feeling a reverential quivering because the higher world cannot

---

[2] "Words of Wisdom" is a 5-volume edition of the Messages of the Masters of Wisdom. You can order books on Amazon or get acquainted with their content on the website http://sirius-eng.net

approach you when you are in towns and even in small settlements. Only in nature, where there are no traces of the so-called civilization, can you come into contact with the higher vibrations of our world.

For many people the vibrations of our world are unbearable. That is why, when they happen to be in nature, they again attempt to deafen themselves with rock music or cigarettes, with alcohol or the smell of fire-roasted meat. Isn't this picture of a widespread pastime in nature known to you?

The whole point is the dissimilarity of vibrations. Many people have tied themselves really tightly to the low vibrations of the physical and the astral planes, so that any time they happen to be in nature the silence becomes a real torture for them…"

From Words of Wisdom Volume 1, May 10, 2005.

"…pay attention to the level of your consciousness during the day. Your consciousness is very mobile. I may say that during the day you continually glide in your consciousness along some scale from its lowest to its highest level. Everything you encounter in life influences the level of your consciousness, including all the people whose auras come into contact with yours, films that you watch and music that you listen to. Literally everything in your world affects you. Thus, your main task is to maintain the level of your consciousness at the highest level available to you for the most part of the day…"

From Words of Wisdom Volume 1, May 14, 2005.

"Many contemporary people surround themselves with the wonders of modern technology, state-of-the-art computers, audio- and video technology, but their level of consciousness remains the same as the level of consciousness of a savage sitting next to a bonfire in a cave and devouring his share of meat under the sounds of a drum or a tambourine.

You can drive the most modern car, wear the most fashionable clothes, but your consciousness will still remain at the same level as that of a cave-dweller.

That is why the Path is much thornier at your time than it has ever been before. You are surrounded by a large number of temptations and it is much easier said than done to maintain a high spiritual level while living in the whirlpool of life in your city jungles.

The entire reality around you has to be transformed. Man has to reveal his Divine potential and become closer to nature. Life itself must become as simple as possible, rich with its inner content but not with outer entertainments that, if one thinks about them, resemble the entertainments of savages. A habit of a contemporary man to cover himself with trinkets is very much akin to the manner in which savages decorated themselves.

You can judge the level of spiritual achievements, spiritual progress or degradation of a person by his manner of dressing, by the music he listens to, by the way of life he prefers…"

From Words of Wisdom Volume 1,
June 3, 2005.

"Soft music and the communication with nature are able to affect the soul of a child much more positively than you can imagine. But when you do not care what music your children listen to and in what company they spend their free time, you cultivate the reasons for your future problems.

Throw away everything unnecessary from your life, the things you can exist without, and you will obtain much free time for your spiritual unfolding, for communications, and for meditations.

The simplest things you can do in your life, which not only do not require big financial expenses but also release you from many of such expenses, are able to bring you to literally revolutionary changes in your life- to the leap in your consciousness..."

From Words of Wisdom Volume 1,
June 15, 2005.

"It is fairly clear that you will not be able to change all circumstances of your life instantly and move to a quiet, secluded place, leaving your established job and family. No, you are not required to do that, but you need to strive for the proper behavior models, for the quiet, charming music, for the gentle rustling of the grass, for the prattling of the birds and gentle babbling of the water. When the proper models of music, films, paintings, and everything that surrounds you fill your consciousness and your closest company, then you will be able to gradually overcome the negative effects of your world and transition into another, subtle world.

Your transition into the subtle world will be assured when you are able to assure the presence of the subtle world in your inner space and in your outer space. Then the angels and elementals will be able to come visit you, and you will be able to see them with your regular human eyes. Everything is in your power, and everything can be achieved through the change of your consciousness, gradually, step by step. Yet, all the steps that you take should be made in the right direction. That is what constitutes the difficulty, as the majority of you forget on the following day about all your good intentions and plans that you have made in your head while reading the dictations of the Masters..."

From Words of Wisdom Volume 2, July 16, 2006.

"...for the majority of people, it is becoming clear already that neither alcohol, nor music that is destructive for the surrounding environment, nor past hobbies give them satisfaction. The search for something new is becoming wider and wider.

You are given recommendations on how to protect yourselves from the influence of everything that brings low vibrations. When you are able to bring the Divine models into your life, you will be able to feel fulfillment and harmony. Of course, not all people are able to strive for the proper models. That is a natural and legitimate stage at which there will simultaneously be people with such different levels of vibrations, that when they meet each other in the street, they will perceive each other as aliens.

The mix of the good and the bad on Earth has to be sorted gradually. The process of sifting out the ashes from cinders is taking place in the Divine thresher.

And you are living now during this time. That is why it is very difficult for you. However, this process has a beginning and an end, as does everything in the physical world..."

From Words of Wisdom Volume 2, July 3, 2007.

"You are very sensitive beings. Your subtle bodies, when attuned to the Higher worlds, are like a Stradivarius violin. However, many of you prefer to drive nails with that violin. Imagine a real Stradivarius violin. Generations of people have been enjoying its charming sounds. You are taught to recognize its value as a true piece of art. Why do you value yourselves less than a violin? You are much better conduits of the energies of the subtle plane. You are capable of transmitting the energies of the Higher worlds into your world. However, you treat the material things of your world with much greater respect than you treat yourselves.

Your unwillingness to listen to yourselves and keep yourselves in purity is related to your psychological problems; and the lack of love for yourselves lies at the root of these problems of yours. You need to love yourselves, not as a physical body, but as the manifestation of God on Earth. You are a part of God, and you should take care of all your bodies and maintain them purely as a manifestation of the Divine.

All your bodies need proper care. Your physical body must receive proper nutrition. The higher the vibrations of the food, the less food you need to eat.

Your emotional body needs food in the form of the subtle energies that come from the Higher worlds. Your emotional body constantly needs to feed on the subtle energy. You try to satisfy the hunger of your emotional body by feeding it with surrogates consisting of low-quality music and television programs. You litter your emotional body by constantly putting it in the unfavorable conditions that exist in your world. Try to protect yourselves from the sounds that come from all directions. One hour a day of listening to the radio or watching television is enough to deprive you of communication with the Higher worlds for one month..."

From Words of Wisdom Volume 2, July 4 2007.

"Legislative measures must be taken toward those who are trying to upset the world with the sounds of ragged rhythms. Each of those who like to listen to rock music, or to any kind of music with improper rhythms, lowers the vibration of the surrounding space many miles around. This hooliganism must be stopped.

While the alcohol that you drink and the cigarette that you smoke lower only your own vibrations and the vibrations of the people who live together with you, the pounding music affects thousands of people. If you knew about the consequences of such hooliganism for your lower bodies, the first thing you would do would be to prohibit your children from to listening to such music forever.

There are very simple measures that allow you to quickly raise the vibrations on the physical plane, and one of these measures is the prohibition of listening to loud music..."

From Words of Wisdom Volume 2, July 4, 2007.

"The situation is that it literally depends on each of you how the process of changing will happen. Earth, as well as each of you, is in a very difficult situation now. Earth is experiencing awful overstrain connected with the impact of the so-called civilization of yours. Imagine, how Earth and the elementals, who maintain the order on Earth and look after the planet feel, bearing all that violence over nature which is committed in your world.

Only the influence of one loudspeaker, working at high volume, spreading the irregular beat of rock music, is enough for thousands of elementals to be shocked, and instead of fulfilling their duties connected with keeping the order on the planet, they become ill or even die.

You should think not only about yourself. It is your duty to care about those inhabitants of planet Earth who evolve on the subtle plane. Think about the example that you show to your younger brothers, not to mention the fact that you should think deeply about the example that you show to your own children. None of your actions or words passes away without a trace..."

From Words of Wisdom Volume 3,
December 22, 2007.

"Gradually, zones that are free of rock music and any manifestations of mass consciousness will form on Earth. Gradually, there will be more and more such corners. With time, the mere vibrations of such places will scare away any non-divine manifestations. Now, think about how you can create such isles of Divine manifestations in the material world. Think about what you personally can do in order to create such a corner, such a settlement..."

From Words of Wisdom Volume 3, June 24, 2008.

"Remember that energy is flowing in the direction of your attention. Therefore, always try to direct this energy at creating the right patterns in your world. The fruits won't take long to show on the physical plane of the planet Earth.

You should control every erg of the Divine energy. That is why the withdrawal of non-divine manifestations from your consciousness and your environment is being brought into the foreground. These can be pictures, films, games, and music, including wrong non-divine vibrations..."

From Words of Wisdom Volume 3,
January 1, 2009.

"... the promotion of the right models in all spheres of life can pull humankind out of the swamp of fears, idleness, despondency, and depression. There are so many true models in all areas of art. There are so many true systems of upbringing and education. You just need to have enlightened leadership at the state or even at the local level for these true patterns to have wide application. Do not indulge the lowest human instincts. In that way we create the most undesirable future for our descendants.

Only the patterns of light, only beauty should take the first place in all media, and especially on television and on the Internet. Everything can still be corrected! Devotees of Spirit are needed! Creators and builders are needed!..."

From Words of Wisdom Volume 4,
December 4, 2009.

This material was prepared by Tatyana N. Mickushina. City of Omsk, Russia.

References:

Tatyana N. Mickushina. *Words of Wisdom. Messages of the Ascended Masters.* Volumes 1-5, 2017.

About Love
and sexual energy

Tatyana N. Mickushina

This book tells us about the most elevated feeling of Love – Divine Love.

This book also contains the forgotten ancient knowledge on the use of sexual energy, which by following this advice you can improve your own health and that of your family as well as facilitate prosperity and well-being.

This book is intended for the attention of a broad reading audience.

Divine Love and earthly love. What is the difference between them?

Is sex love?

Think whether the degradation of moral standards that exists in our society, is harmless.

How to become a source of the perfect feeling of Love?

Secrets of Music

A collection of articles

Translator: Natasha Zwanck

Please, leave your review about this book at amazon.com. This will greatly help in spreading the Teaching of the Ascended Masters given through the Messenger Tatyana Mickushina.

Buy Books by Tatyana N. Mickushina on Amazon:
amazon.com/author/tatyana_mickushina